# Table of Contents

S0-ASC-217

# A Wonderful Idea

You probably don't think twice about heading off to the park on a Saturday to ride your bike or play a game of soccer. But if you had been growing up in the 1850s, you couldn't have done that. You couldn't even have found a small playground with some climbing bars!

This city street from long ago was bustling with so much activity, people had a hard time just taking a walk! What do you think about the traffic rules on this street?

Back in those days, there were no places for recreation, such as **public** parks or playgrounds, anywhere in the United States. People living in crowded cities had no place to go to be outdoors and enjoy nature.

Then a man named Frederick Law Olmsted had a wonderful idea. This is the story of how his idea became reality, and how it helped change the way people lived.

Frederick Law Olmsted grew up in the early 1800s. As a child, he loved nature and spent much of his time outdoors. Together, he and his father would tour scenic places in New England. When he was 14 years old, he got a bad case of sumac poisoning, which is similar to poison ivy. It threatened to damage his eyesight and prevented him from going to college.

Still, Frederick studied on his own and grew up to be an active young man with many interests. At one time, he was a farmer. Then he worked on a merchant ship, traveling to China. Later, he was a reporter for a New York newspaper, writing against slavery in the American South. But his greatest interest was nature.

Olmsted liked to visit the Adirondack Mountains in New York because of their spectacular scenery.

People went to this English park, with its open meadows, trees, and lakes, to get a taste of nature. Why do you think Olmsted would like such a place?

When Frederick visited England as a young man, he spent some time in the city of Birkenhead. He was thrilled to see the public park there. He loved the open, inviting feeling of this place, with its vast meadows dotted with trees.

As he watched residents of the city, young and old, enjoying their park, he became very excited. He thought that the beauty and peacefulness of such a place could calm and soothe people who lived in busy, noisy cities.

Frederick's visit gave him an idea. He became determined to create parks like this one for people in his own country. He would soon get his chance.

# A Backyard for a Big City

Central Park was the first public park developed in the United States. Frederick Law Olmsted helped to design it. But building this park took time, money, and a lot of hard work.

# A Crowded City of Immigrants

In the 1850s, New York City was already a very crowded city. Hundreds of **immigrants** were arriving daily from other countries. Many of these people lived in **tenements**, poorly built buildings that often lacked proper sanitation and comforts such as heat and hot water. Some people lived in small wooden shanties, or huts.

The city was dirty. The air was **polluted** with soot from the coal that everyone burned to heat their homes. There were no places to see green trees, to walk on grass, or to smell flowers. New York City needed a "backyard"!

In a tenement, a large family might live together in one small room.

# Wanted: A Park for People

The need for a park became the **issue** of the day. People talked and argued about it. Newspaper articles were written about it. Finally, the leaders of the city agreed to build a large public park where there would be trees, lakes, and meadows. In 1857, the Central Park Commission was formed to direct the building of the park.

That same year, at an inn, Olmsted met one of the park **commissioners.** Olmsted spoke about his ideas for building a public park. He described Birkenhead Park that had so excited him in England a few years before.

Formal gardens like this one were popular at the time. How is this garden different from what you would find in nature?

Builders did not want to build houses on the swampy site. So the commission thought it was a good place to turn into a park.

The commissioner was so fascinated, he suggested that Olmsted apply for the job of superintendent for the new park. Fortunately, Olmsted got the job. He would be in charge of the workers who were brought in to start clearing the park **site.**

The site for the new park was an area of more than 700 acres (about the size of 500 football fields) in the center of Manhattan. But it was mostly swampland and covered with huge rocks. Not only that, on the land there were pigsties and **slaughterhouses,** where animals were butchered for food.

Sadly, there were more than 1,600 people living in shanties on the site. The shanties would have to come down, and the people would have to move. When they resisted, the police were called in. Everyone living on the site was forced to leave. Only some received money for their land.

Now the city had a site for a park. But what exactly would the park look like?

## The Contest

The Central Park Commission announced a contest. The best design would be used for the park. This contest was the idea of Calvert Vaux, an English-born architect who also loved the idea of a public park. Vaux knew Olmsted, and the two men decided to design an entry for the contest together.

Olmsted and Vaux began sketching their ideas. They designed every acre of the park, deciding where each path, bridge, and group of trees would be placed.

On April 1, 1858, after months of hard work, the partners submitted their plan, which they called Greensward. Four weeks later, the winning plan was announced. It was theirs!

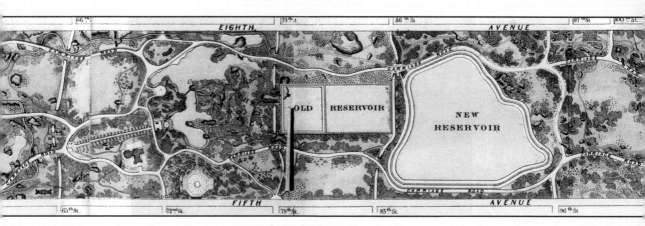

Compare this plan of Greensward with the photo of Central Park on page 12. What looks the same? What's different? What do you think would surprise Olmsted and Vaux if they could see the photo on page 12?

## Building the Park

The building of Central Park was a huge task. It took more than 20,000 workers and about 20 years to complete. In 1858, there was very little machinery to move huge rocks or to drain swamps.

The task had to be done with horses and manpower. Workmen used pickaxes, shovels, and even gunpowder for blasting rocks. Olmsted and Vaux could be seen up to the tops of their boots in mud, directing the job.

The pigsties and slaughterhouses were torn down. Tons of fresh **topsoil** were brought in by truck from New Jersey. More than four million trees, shrubs and other plants were carefully set into the soil.

As the prize-winning plan of Olmsted and Vaux slowly took shape, a wonderful place came to life. There were paths and bridges for walking, and four man-made lakes for boating in summer or ice skating in winter.

Many Irish and German immigrants were hired to work on the construction site for Central Park.

Underpasses helped make the park a safe place for children to play.

And Olmsted and Vaux came up with a new idea—roadways called **underpasses** through the park. This way, horse-and-carriage traffic wouldn't get in the way of the views. Everywhere visitors might look, they would be able to see peaceful, rolling parkland.

The center of Manhattan was transformed from a muddy, rocky swamp into a park so beautiful that it still enchants visitors today. Part of Olmsted's brilliance is that he designed Central Park to look just like nature. In fact, many visitors think that it was *always* there. They don't realize that the park is man-made.

# A National Park for America

Spectacular! Astonishing! Exquisite! These are the words that people use to describe Yosemite National Park. Visitors marvel at its soaring mountain peaks and giant sequoia trees, its glistening streams and waterfalls.

Yosemite National Park is in the Sierra Nevada Mountains of California. It covers almost 1,200 square miles. Because the area has been named a national park by the United States government, it is protected. No one can use the land for farming, mining, or resorts. No one can hunt there. No one can destroy the land's natural beauty.

Back in 1863, though, when Frederick Law Olmsted first saw Yosemite Valley, it was not a national park. No area of the United States had yet been protected in this way. Still, news about this special place had spread. Tourists from all over the world were coming to see Yosemite.

People who knew they could make money from tourism started building hotels and houses there. They cut down trees and started planting fruit orchards. The balance of plant and animal life in Yosemite was threatened. If this continued, Yosemite would be doomed.

Many kinds of animals live in Yosemite, including mountain lions, bears, and deer.

## Taking Action

Olmsted wanted to conserve, or save, the incredible beauty of Yosemite. You could say that he was one of the very first **conservationists.** So when he saw how people were treating the land, he decided to speak out.

In 1864, Olmsted wrote a long report to the U.S. Congress in Washington, D.C., stating his reasons why the Yosemite Valley should be protected by the state of California. He also said that it was the duty of a national government to make natural scenery available to all its citizens.

The sequoias of Mariposa Grove can grow to heights of 100 meters and live for thousands of years. They provide homes for many kinds of animals.

Olmsted's report was introduced to Congress by Senator John Conness of California. Other people voiced their support of Yosemite, too. Then, on June 30, 1864, President Abraham Lincoln signed a bill making Yosemite Valley and Mariposa Grove a public park.

For the first time ever, the United States government had set aside lands to protect them and to allow people to enjoy them. Olmsted was named one of the first commissioners to manage the park.

How do you think Olmsted's ideas for Yosemite Park and Central Park were similar?

Visitors enjoy rafting in Yosemite, which became a national park in 1890.

# Living Outside the City

Another way for people to be closer to nature was to live outside the city. By the 1860s, there were more railways in our country and better and faster trains. These trains made it possible for people to move to **suburbs.** Americans could now live in homes on larger pieces of land, and they could commute to work in nearby cities.

The suburbs were quiet, but their design was very rigid. Most designers of suburban communities used a straight **grid** pattern for laying out the streets.

If there were rivers, or hills and rock formations, town planners either ignored them or had them removed. And no public parks existed there. Some people had their own private parks, but these were fenced in. Houses were often built close to the road, so there were few grassy lawns.

## A New Kind of Suburb

By 1868, Olmsted and Vaux had become well known for their work on Central Park. Now, for the first time, they were hired to design an entire suburb. This suburb, called Riverside, was to be built on 1,600 acres of land, nine miles west of Chicago, Illinois.

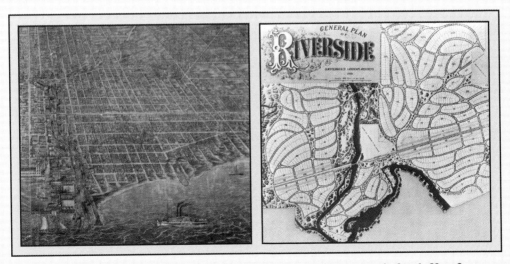

How does the plan for the city of Chicago (shown at left) differ from the plan for Riverside?

Olmsted used his ideas about park design to create a natural setting for the new town. One of the first things he noticed was that Riverside was located right on the Des Plaines River. This was the most beautiful natural feature on the site. What should he do with it?

Olmsted decided to create a huge park along the sloping riverfront and surround it with plants and tall trees. Olmsted and Vaux hoped that all the people of Riverside would enjoy the views of the park and the river.

One of Olmsted's goals was to preserve Riverside's natural beauty. The community has many open areas for rest and enjoyment.

This library was built in Riverside in 1930. Why would Olmsted have thought this was a good spot for it?

This grand park alone would make Riverside look a lot different from earlier suburbs! But Olmsted had other ideas as well. Instead of ignoring natural features, such as hills, he made sure to include every one of them in his plan. Roads were built to curve around hills and waterways.

Olmsted's goal was to plan a community that would look both beautiful and natural. There were unfenced parks scattered throughout Riverside. Each house was built with a 10-meter lawn in front, and trees were planted all along the roads.

People heard about Olmsted and Vaux's exciting plan for Riverside, and soon other cities wanted something like it. In 1868, Olmsted and Vaux designed Parkside in Buffalo, New York. Olmsted then went on to design Belle Isle in Detroit, Michigan, and Druid Hills in Atlanta, Georgia. Each one of these beautiful communities still exists today.

How are these homes in Parkside beautified by nature?

The suburb of Parkside has curving roads, gently sloping hills, and large public parks.

Olmsted felt that the suburbs should be a little like the country. They would be scenic places with parks and homes shaded by trees, so homeowners would be eager to return there after a tiring day in the city. What do you think of this idea? Do you think Olmsted succeeded in his goal?

# Designing the Outdoors

The design of this beautiful Japanese garden is based on a tradition that is thousands of years old. In Japan and many other places in the world, landscape architecture has been practiced for centuries. In ancient Babylonia, people created hanging gardens. Ancient Greek and Roman cities had open spaces set aside for people to gather.

In Europe in the 1600s and 1700s, control over nature was a popular idea. Formal gardens were built with rigid patterns and clipped hedges. Some homes had unusual gardens, with plants shaped to look like animals or other fanciful objects. But by the 1800s, a new idea took hold in England. There, landscapers were designing gardens to look more like natural countryside.

While people have always used nature to beautify their homes and cities, this kind of work was not considered a **profession** until the mid–1800s. In fact, it was Frederick Law Olmsted and Calvert Vaux who came up with the term "**landscape architect**" to describe their job. They felt that what they did was similar to what a building architect does. The difference was that they used things from nature—land, trees, water, and stone—as their building materials instead of wood, concrete, and steel.

Historians think the Hanging Gardens of Babylon may have looked like this. How is nature used here?

This is a model of a new skating rink park. What do you imagine this park will look like when it is built? What kinds of things would you think about if you were planning such a park?

## Landscape Architecture Today

Today, landscape architects still design parks, public gardens, and suburbs, but they also design many other kinds of places, such as college campuses, playgrounds, golf courses, and zoos. They design every part of a site, from stairways to fences, from walls to walkways, and from the arrangement of trees and flowers to the patterns on the pavement. They figure out where to install watering systems and roadways for transportation.

These outdoor planners make sure that natural resources, such as fresh air and sunshine, are considered in their plans. Why do you think these things are important?

Landscape architects still supervise the clearing of sites for housing developments, gardens, and schools. But now, their workers use machinery, such as tractors, bulldozers, cranes, and steam rollers to do most of the heavy work.

**Preserving** history might also be part of a landscape architect's job. For example, the home of a famous person in history might have become worn or damaged by age. A team of landscape architects and builders can restore the home and grounds to make them look the way they did when the owner was alive. In that way, landscape architects not only beautify our present surroundings, they can also help preserve our past.

It's important to preserve the buildings and grounds of Mt. Vernon, George Washington's home. What might the landscape architect have to think about?

# Remembering Frederick Law Olmsted

Olmsted's dream of bringing nature into everyone's lives came true in a big way that surely would have made him proud. Now we have a national park system that includes hundreds of parks, with spectacular land and wildlife that are protected. Most cities and towns in America have at least one park where people can sit and enjoy nature. Thousands of creative people have followed in Olmsted's footsteps and studied to become landscape architects.

Many people think of Frederick Law Olmsted as "the father of American landscape architecture." Why do you think that's true?